THIRD PRINTING

"FOR YOUR OWN UNFORGOTTEN THINGS"

PUBLISHED BY
INSPIRATION HOUSE
SOUTH WINDSOR, CT.

Printed by The Pond-Ekberg Co., Inc., Chicopee, Mass.

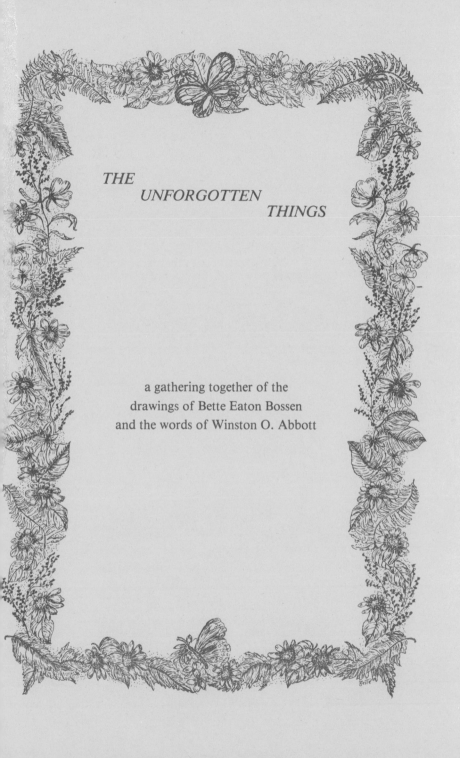

THE
UNFORGOTTEN
THINGS

a gathering together of the
drawings of Bette Eaton Bossen
and the words of Winston O. Abbott

how very significant that the light of stars millions of
miles away should sparkle on the surface of a pond
unnamed and little known —

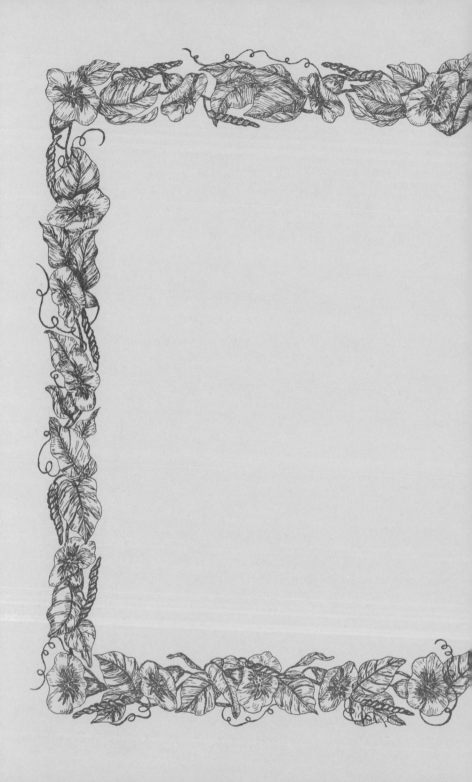

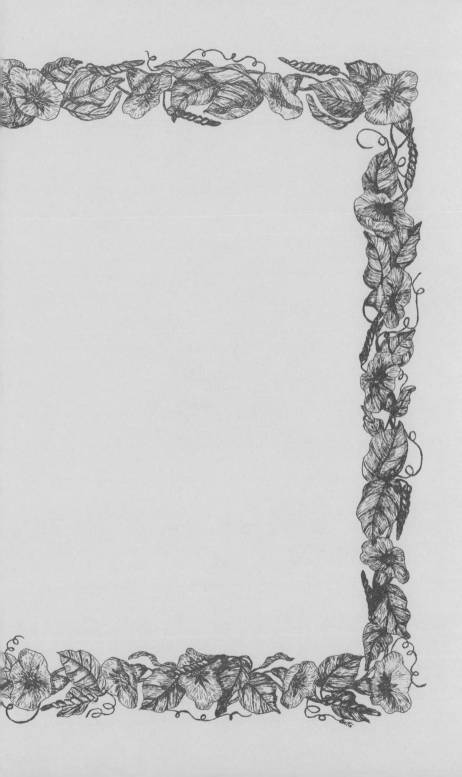

in this hushed and shadowed wood — life is being
transmuted into life —
                            here the tired and weathered
hands of the Creator have found new strength — have
reached down into the moist and moulding earth —
to fashion new forms of life from the residue of
forgotten years —
                            here the changeless is ever changing —
here yesterday mingles for the moment with to-morrow —
if we rest for awhile in this quiet place — we will
share a sense of reverence for the mystery of creation —
            listen —
                            that was the song of the veery —

from the book — Have You Heard The Cricket Song —

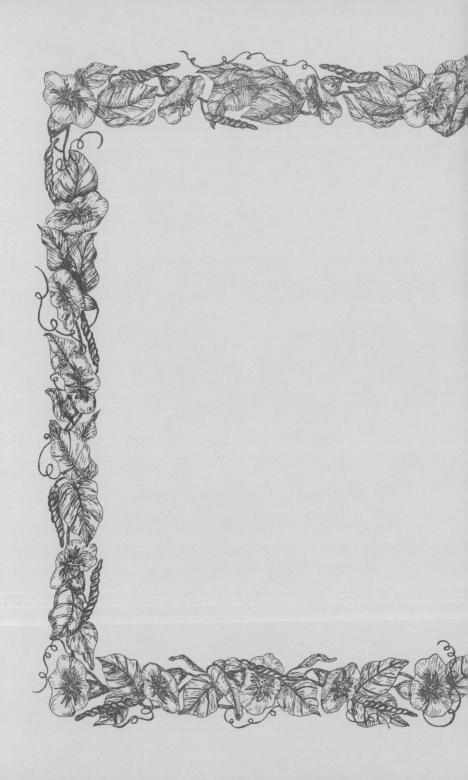

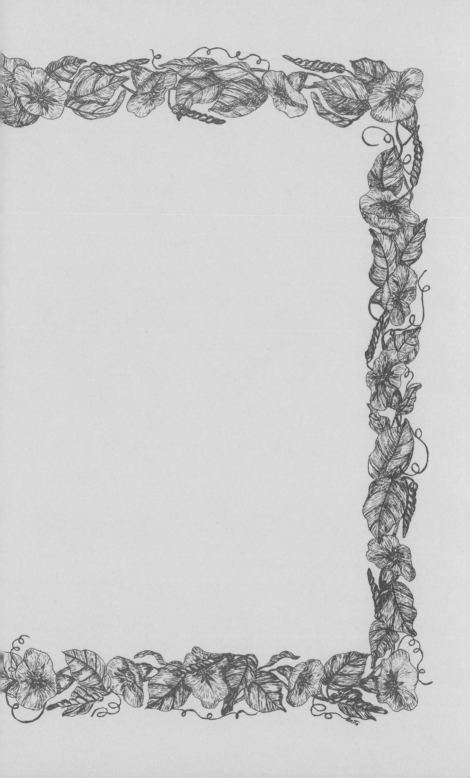

sometimes a moment is greater than eternity —
  that moment when every living thing becomes
  a part of life — when life is truly shared by
  every living thing —

twilight is a time for sharing — and a
time for remembering — remembering the things of
beauty wasted by our careless hands — our frequent
disregard of other living things — the many songs
unheard because we would not listen —
　　　　　　　listen to-night with all the
wisdom of your spirit — listen too with
all the compassion of your heart —
lest there come another night —
when there is only silence —

　　　　　　　　　　　　a great
　　　　　　　　　　　　and
　　　　　　　　　　　　total
　　　　　　　　　　　　silence —

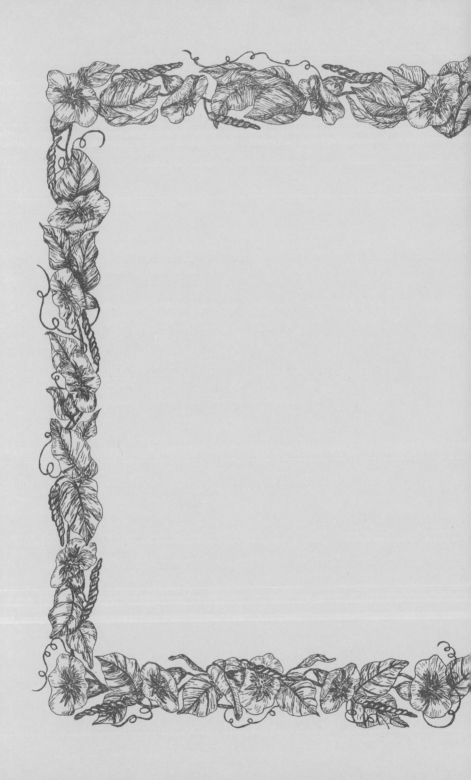

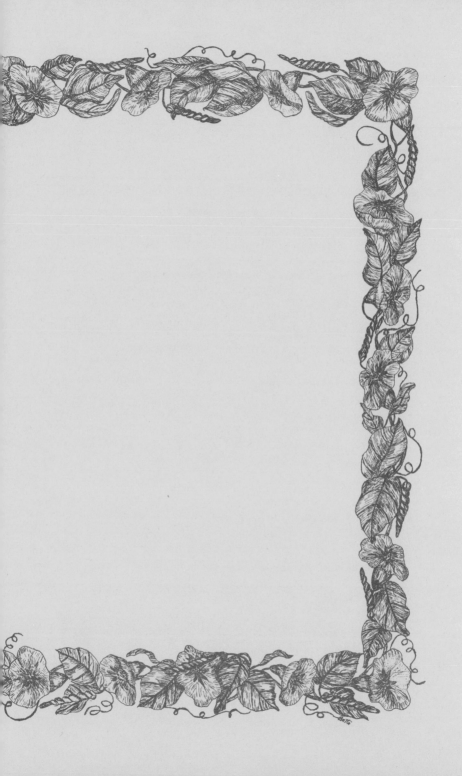

wisdom is as vast and ageless as the sea — but love and
beauty reach beyond its farthest shore —

there are no lines and angles in nature's calendar —
only gentle curves that reach around the seasons
and return to the place of their beginning —

                                      I have
tried to live by the warmth of summer and the chill
of winter — by the bright sadness that is autumn
and the resurgence that is spring —

                               and if I fail —
there are rare moments like this night — when I am
able to reach beyond the restriction of man's
calendar —

                  to touch — if ever so briefly — the mystery
and the majesty of the changing seasons — and
perhaps — catch a fleeting glimpse of the beauty of
eternity as it sweeps across the hill —

     from the book — Letters From Chickadee Hill —

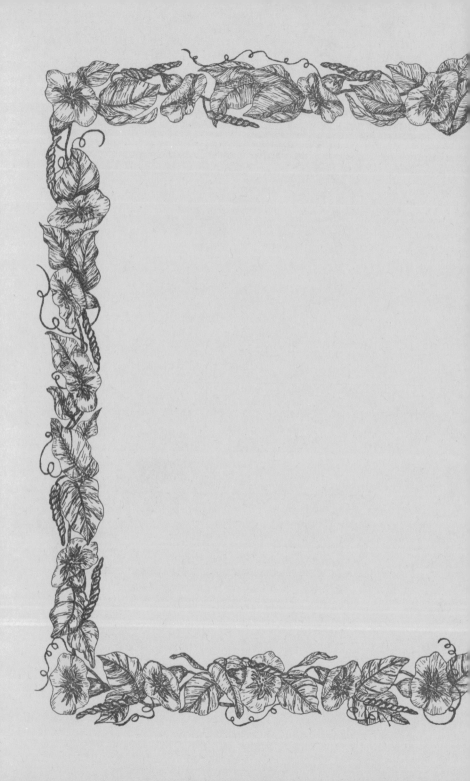

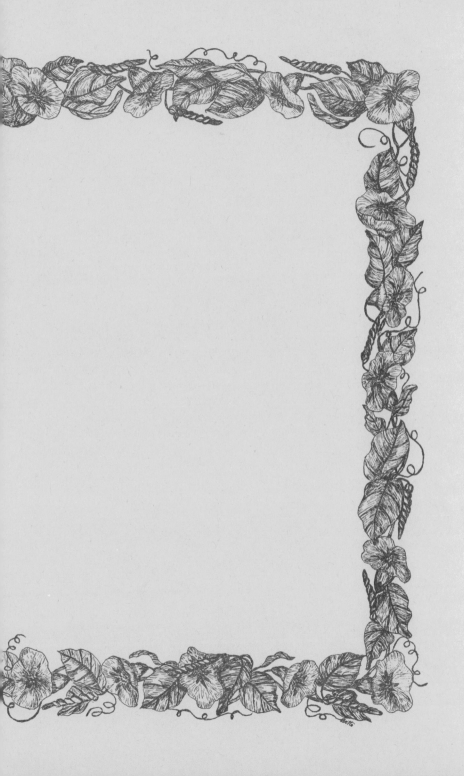

each bird designs its nest according to its needs — and never
to copy or outdo its neighbor — and I find this refreshing
of itself —

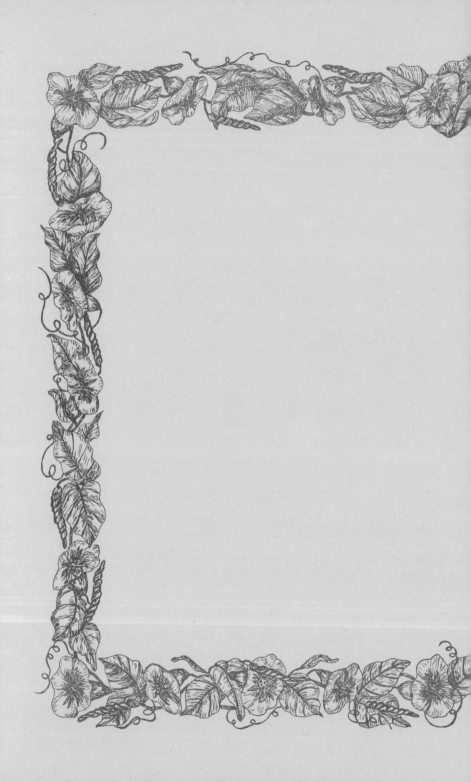

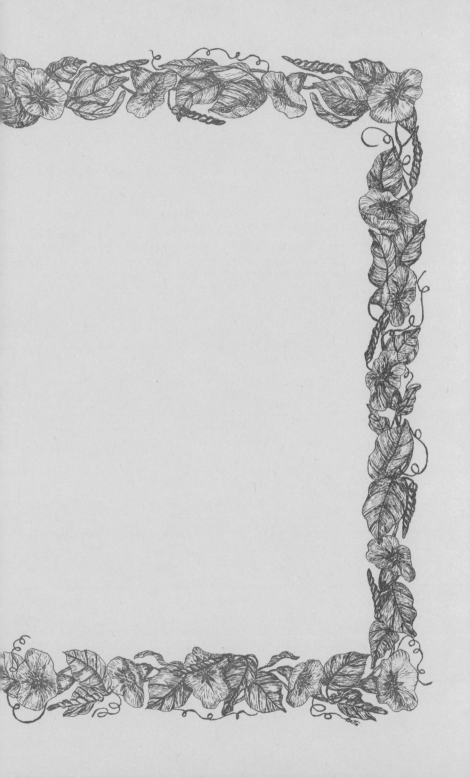

I wonder if the emerging butterfly — spreading its fragile
and trembling wings after a long winter sleep — will ever
know that long months before — it was a creature of lesser
beauty —

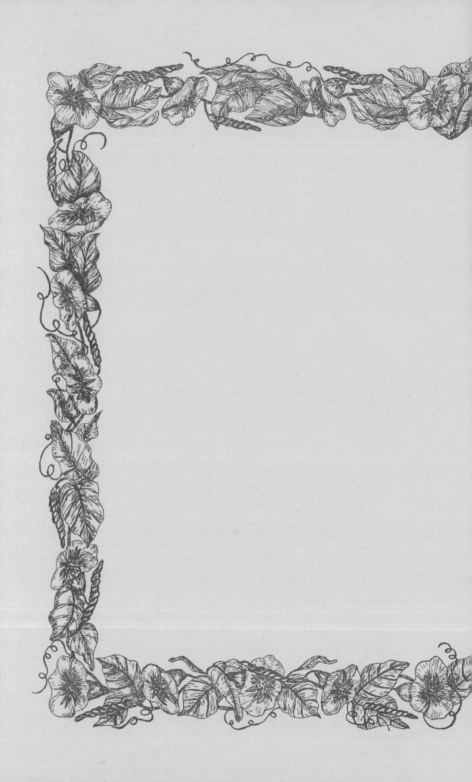

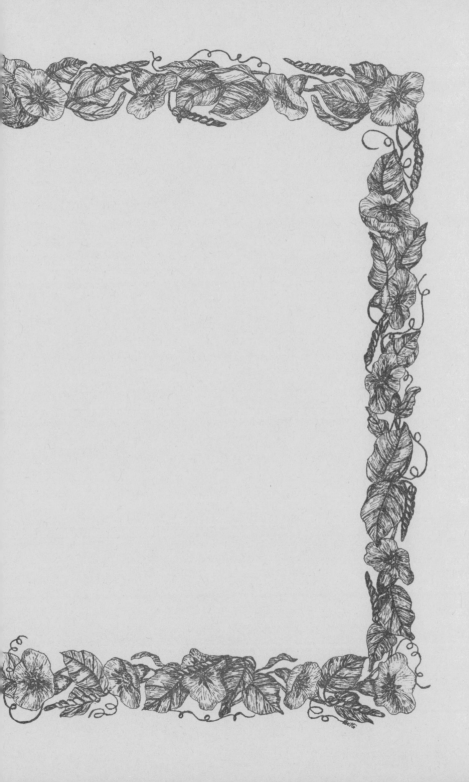

there can be no rainbow until the storm has passed —

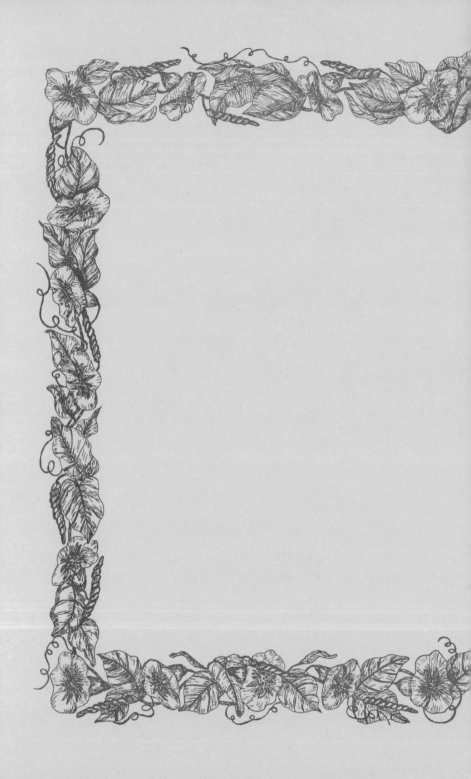

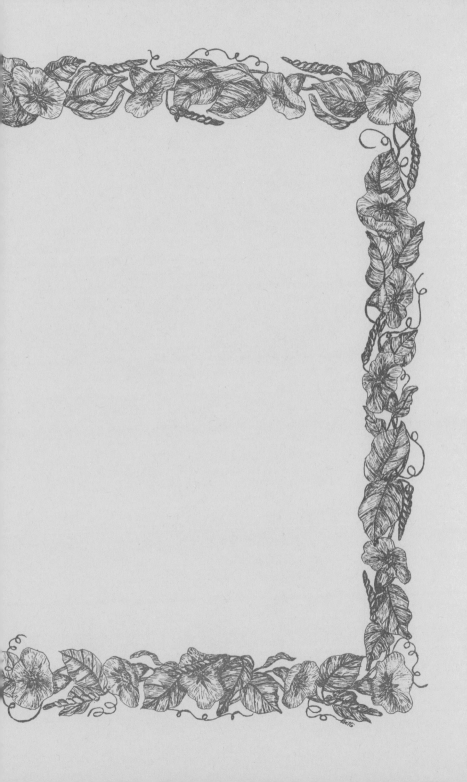

it is the sense of mystery that gives to life
its majesty —
　　　　　　　　for it comes — it goes — it is the
song of bird upon the branch — it is the silence
when the song is gone —
　　　　　　　　　　it is as fragile as a
spark before the wind — and yet its light may rise
to be another star —
　　　　　　　　　　it is the radiance of the
dawn — and the mysterious pathway to the dark —
　　　　　　　　　　　　　　　　　and
it is not always easy to remember — that the
scattered embers of the afterglow —
　　　　　　　　　　　　　are banked by
some invisible hand —
　　　　　　　　　to light the fires of sunrise
in another day —

　　from the book — Come Climb My Hill —

if you remember a single blossom that defied the frost —
you have no reason to fear this great mystery that is life —
for you hold its secret deep within your heart —

if you will listen with your heart — you too will know —
that a raindrop is part of the sea — and the sea is
contained in a raindrop —

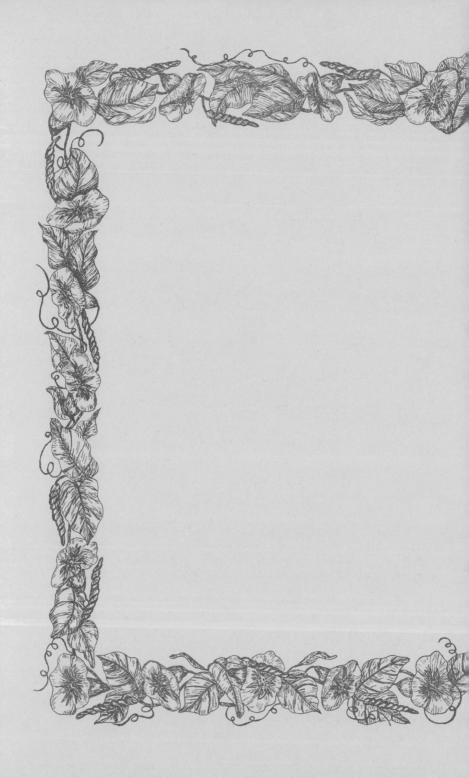

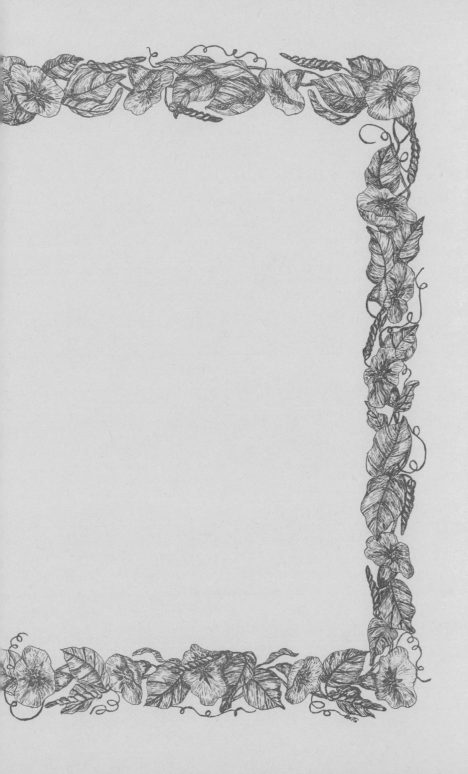

the future is borne upon the wind —

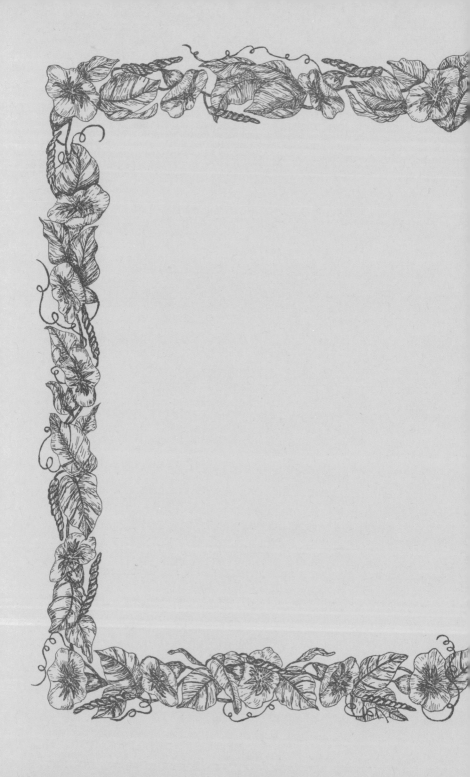

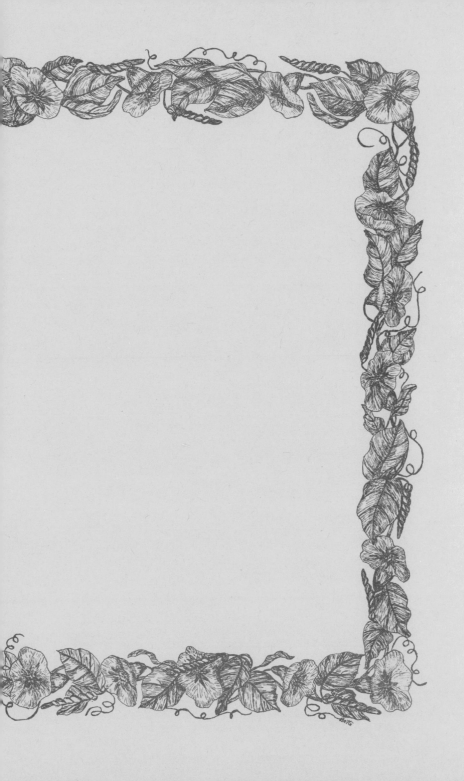

we call them weeds and pass them by — but they are
friends of bird and bee and butterfly —

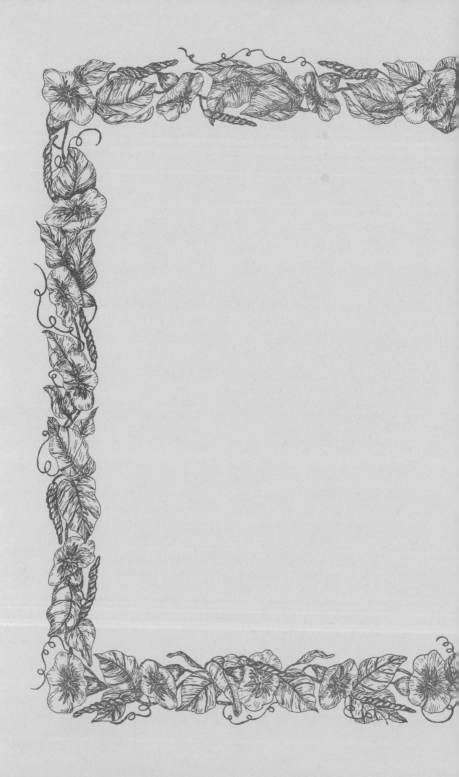

how tiny are the lamps of fireflies moving in
the scented dusk — how feeble are their lights
where lightning marks the brooding storm —

                                           how
feeble are their lights —
                  and then the drenching
rains put out their lamps —
                      but soon the rains
will go to other meadows — and the grasses will
struggle to free themselves from the sodden
earth — and the tiny lamps will be lighted once
again and move undaunted through the dripping
darkness —
                  can a tiny insect know that this night
will have no other light until the stars return —

     from the book — Sing With The Wind —

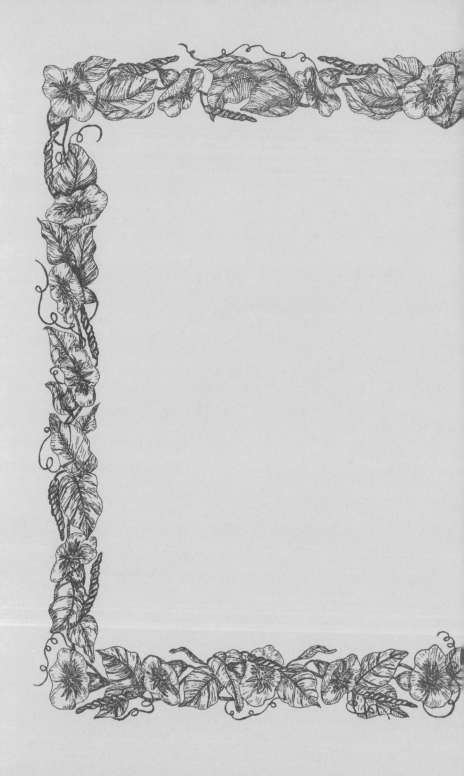

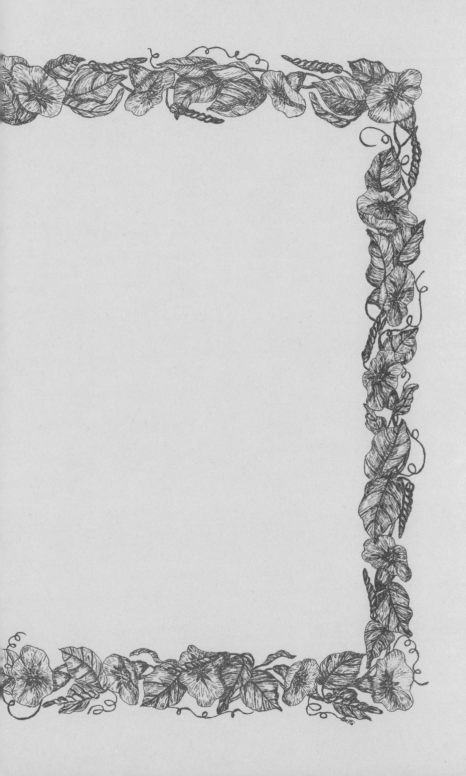

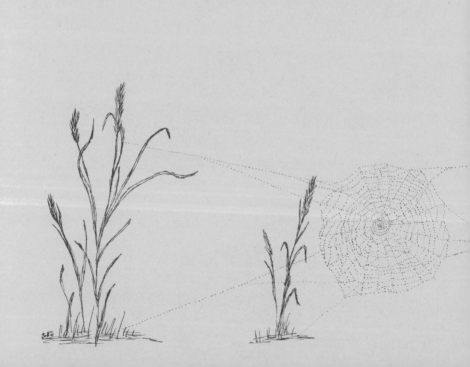

there is strength in gentleness — and there is gentleness
in strength —

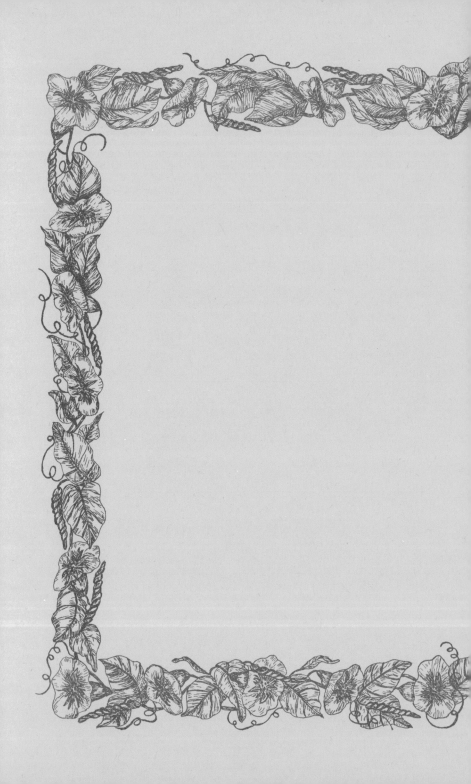

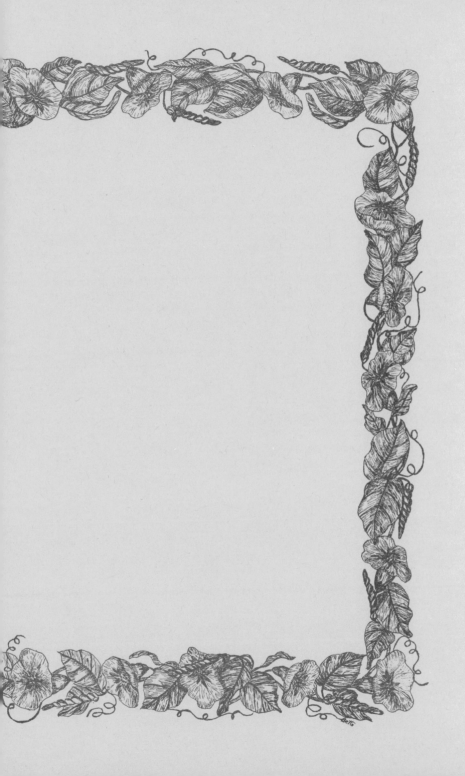

live slowly through each fleeting day — for time is of
man's own dreaming —

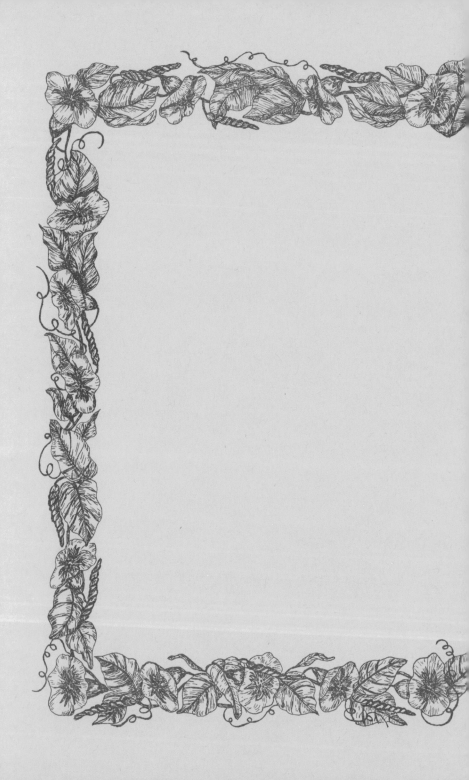

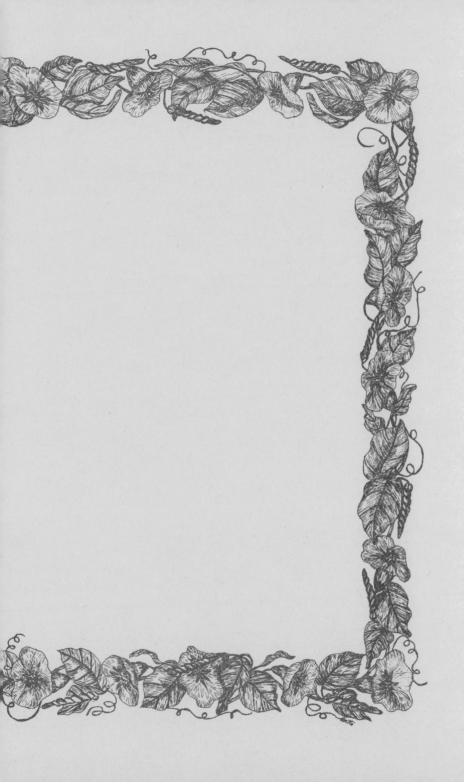

beauty often sleeps in a quiet heart — and patiently waits to be born again —

each living thing has need of
other living things — depends
upon and is depended upon —

my gift of life is a thing of transient beauty —
a thing of mystery — and above all else a miracle —
it is a thing of beauty because of the soul — a
mystery because it stretches between the invisible
yesterday and the unknown to-morrow — a miracle
because it is a composite of countless other lives —
                                          from many lives
I have gathered courage and strength — I have learned
humility and gentleness and forgiveness —

                                          and for
all of these blessings I am grateful —

                                          and so you
must understand that your life is not your own —
it has become a part of mine — and so it follows
that my life does not belong to me —

                                          it is yours —

from the book — Come Walk Among The Stars —

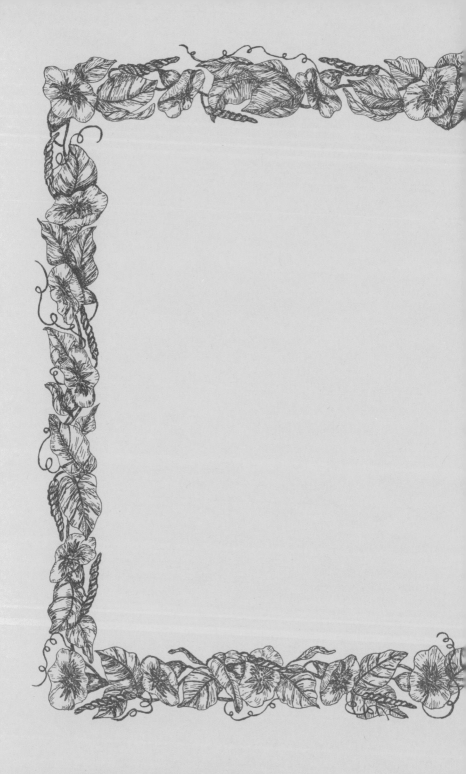

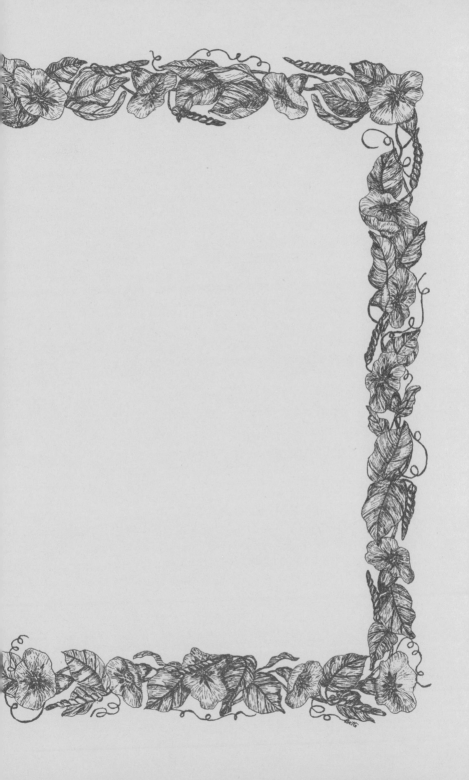

if but once you have touched the hand of the Creator —
there is music in the croaking of the frog —

a cricket song — like a memory — grows more beautiful and meaningful each time it brushes against the night —

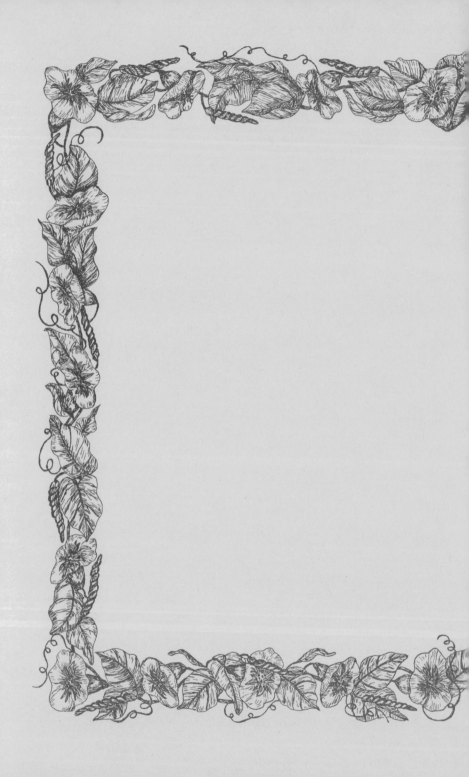

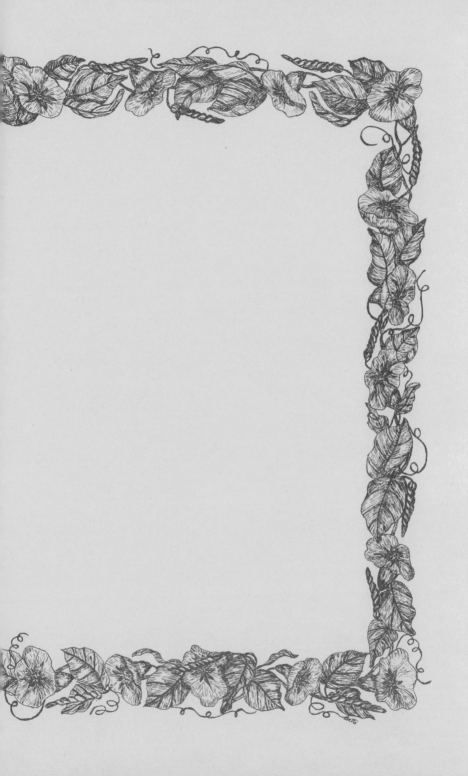

time cannot be measured in the presence of the stars —

the days drift downward as the falling leaves — and are
gone — it is getting late — so very late — and we have yet
to listen to the song of the cricket —